SETTLE & CARLISLE
STEAM FINALE

Michael S Welch

RUNPAST PUBLISHING

© Michael S Welch 1999

Published by Runpast Publishing, 10 Kingscote Grove, Cheltenham, Gloucestershire GL51 6JX

Typesetting and reproduction by Viners Wood Associates – 01452 812813
Printed in England by The Amadeus Press Ltd., Huddersfield

ISBN 1 870754 48 4

Front cover photograph: The Settle & Carlisle line is a paradise for railway pictures, with the route's breathtaking, unsurpassed scenery providing a multitude of excellent photographic locations. One of the best is the viaduct at the head of Mallerstang Common, which carries the line across Ais Gill beck. This viaduct, which is located just a mile north of the summit, is of four arches and was constructed in 1873. It is officially known as 'Bridge No.137', but to many it is simply one of the best photographic spots on the line and, arguably, in Great Britain. In this picture LMSR Class 5MT No.45254, in quite disgraceful external condition, crosses the viaduct with a southbound freight on 30th April 1966, and leaves a thick pall of smoke across the countryside. *Derek Penney*

Back cover photograph: A barren, but magnificent, landscape of fells and bare moorland stretches in all directions as far as the eye can see, in this picture of 'Jubilee' 4-6-0 No.45593 *Kolhapur* approaching Ais Gill summit with the 9.20 SO St Pancras to Glasgow train on 19th August 1967, a typically hazy Pennine summer's day. Between Garsdale and Ais Gill the railway crosses a watershed, from which tributaries flow to the River Ouse on the east and the River Lune, on the west coast. In addition, the source of the River Eden, which eventually reaches the sea near Carlisle, is also in the vicinity. *Peter Fitton*

Title page photograph: Judicious use of a telephoto lens emphasises the constant battle of man and machine against the testing grades of the Settle & Carlisle line, which was definitely not a route for faint-hearted enginemen, or 'clapped-out' locomotives. When this dramatic shot of 'Black Five' No.44902 passing Ais Gill's up distant signal was taken on 18th October 1967, the engine had been climbing almost continuously since leaving Carlisle, nearly forty miles northwards, but at last the crew had the summit in their sight, and could now relax as the really hard work was over. Just over two months later, the magnificent spectacle of real working steam such as this was consigned to the history books. *Neville Simms*

INTRODUCTION

Few lines have had so much written about them as the Settle & Carlisle line, and it seems that every possible accolade has been bestowed on this celebrated railway route. Incomparable, stunning, breathtaking, dramatic and unrivalled are the superlatives that have been used to describe its scenic qualities. It is a wonder that the line was ever completed across such an inhospitable wilderness, and the late Bishop Eric Treacy, surely the doyen of all Settle & Carlisle photographers, once opined that there were three man-made marvels in the north of England – York Minster, Hadrian's Wall and the Settle & Carlisle line, and who would dare to question his judgement?

My own love affair with the Settle & Carlisle line began as late as 1965, when I was returning from Scotland to my holiday base in Manchester. Rather than use a West Coast line express from Carlisle, I decided to catch the 4.37pm local train to Bradford, from where direct trains ran to Manchester. Unfortunately, most of the line was traversed in darkness, but I had seen enough to convince me that Settle & Carlisle was certainly an exceptional line and vowed to return. During subsequent visits I was privileged to see the last 'Jubilees' working over the route, and witness a 'clapped-out' 8F flogging its heart out on the climb to Ais Gill. I have always considered that the sight and sound of a heavy freight doing battle with the 1 in 100 grade past Mallerstang Common at a little more than walking pace, was one of the truly great, unbeatable British steam experiences, though possibly not for the crew of an engine that was shy of steam! The night freights at this location, with the locomotive's blast echoing back from the empty, surrounding fells and shattering the still night air must have been an even more memorable experience. My expeditions to the Settle & Carlisle were often sabotaged by diabolical weather conditions of course, but when the mist lifted and the rain cleared, the sun would break through to reveal a sparkling landscape of unparalleled natural beauty.

This album is intended as a tribute to the final years of 'real' working steam along the Settle & Carlisle route. Compilation of this book has occupied almost three years, mainly due to the fact that the line was comparatively little photographed in colour in BR days, so much detective work was necessary to locate suitable material. Most railway photographers, understandably, preferred the Shap route due to its greater traffic density, and the irresistible, almost magnetic, attraction of the 'Princess Coronation' Pacifics. So, my thanks are offered to all those people who had the foresight to take colour pictures on the Settle & Carlisle line, and who have been kind enough to loan their precious transparencies for publication in this album. In addition, I would like to record my appreciation to David J. Fakes and Graham Mallinson who kindly checked the manuscript, although I accept responsibility for any errors which have crept through. Tom Heavyside, Derek Huntriss and Pete Shaw suggested worthwhile sources of material, without which the selection of pictures would have been much less comprehensive. The illustrations are generally arranged in journey order, starting at Hellifield. Lastly, the technical quality of some of the older pictures, which were taken long before colour photography became commonplace, is not to the standard I would have wished, but many are 'gems' and have been included due to their exceptional historical interest.

M.S.W. Burgess Hill, West Sussex. 22nd April 1999

A scene at Hellifield station in June 1965 as LMSR Class 7P 'Patriot' 4-6-0 No.45530 *Sir Frank Ree* charges through the station at the head of a northbound freight train. By this time only two 'Patriots' – the other was No.45531 *Sir Frederick Harrison* – remained in traffic, and No.45530 was destined to become the final survivor of its class, lasting until December 1965. Originally, Hellifield was served by a small Midland Railway station about 1/2 mile south of the present one, but when the Lancashire & Yorkshire Railway (L&YR) opened their line from Chatburn on 1st June 1880 a new joint station, located immediately north of the junction, was brought into use on the same day. The L&YR line gave access to Lancashire towns via Blackburn. The period between 1901 and 1914 was undoubtedly the heyday of Hellifield station. In 1910 it was handling some 90 passenger trains daily, including through expresses from London to Scotland over the Settle & Carlisle line, trains off the L&YR line and those on the Carnforth and Lancaster routes. Through portions from Liverpool and Manchester to Scotland were provided, so the large amount of shunting required meant that Hellifield was a constant hive of activity. At this time the station had sixty uniformed staff on its payroll. Sadly, the fortunes of Hellifield station gradually declined and today it is an unstaffed halt, but at least the magnificent buildings survive, and have been recently restored.

Jim Winkley

A study of 'Princess Coronation' Pacific No.46238 *City of Carlisle* pausing at Hellifield with the Railway Correspondence and Travel Society's 'North Eastern Railtour' on 27th September 1963. This was the first day of a marathon five-day tour which started from York, and subsequently visited numerous branch lines in the north-east of England, including those to Consett, Rothbury and Barnard Castle. No.46238 hauled the train from Skipton to Carlisle but, despite the very modest load, made an undistinguished run to the Border City, arriving five minutes late. Hellifield station consisted of an island platform with bays at each end and the principal buildings are visible above the train. Part of the motive power depot can be seen on the extreme left of the picture. Hellifield station was an isolated railway junction, serving a small community, most of whom worked on the railway! Note the fields located immediately beyond the boundary of the railway's property, which bear testament to Hellifield's rural location. *D. Tyreman*

A 'Royal Scot', No.46145 *The Duke of Wellington's Regt. (West Riding)* from Holbeck shed, Leeds, awaits the 'right away' from the guard before resuming its journey northwards with 'The Waverley' express to Edinburgh. No.46145 became a regular sight on Anglo-Scottish trains at Hellifield following its transfer from Longsight to Holbeck in early 1953. It remained there until October 1961, when it was officially moved to Low Moor. Actually No.46145 went to Farnley Junction shed for storage, and it never worked regularly again. It was eventually withdrawn in late 1962, and broken-up at Crewe Works during the following year. The principal daytime service between London and Edinburgh was originally named 'The Thames-Forth Express', but this title disappeared when the Second World War broke out in 1939. The name 'The Waverley', which was bestowed upon the 9.15am St. Pancras to Edinburgh train in 1957, was short-lived. In 1964/65 'The Waverley' ceased to run in the wintertime as a separate train. In the winter 'The Thames-Clyde Express' conveyed an Edinburgh portion and also made additional stops to compensate for the withdrawal of 'The Waverley'. This resulted in the former's journey time to Glasgow being considerably lengthened, to 6hr. 50min., compared to the fastest time of 6hr. 30min. at the turn of the century! 'The Waverley' ceased to run in the late 1960s when the Carlisle to Edinburgh route was sadly closed. This picture was taken in 1958.

Neil Thexton

BR Standard Class 4MT 4-6-0 No.75051 is depicted apparently shunting some Civil Engineer's wagons at Hellifield in March 1966. The scene is, however, dominated by the sizeable MR signal cabin. On the right can be seen part of the engine shed which, like most of the railway installations at Hellifield, dated from the improvements carried out in 1879/80 when the L&YR opened their line from Chatburn. It is recorded that the improved facilities at Hellifield, consisting of a new station complete with refreshment room, engine shed and additional siding accommodation cost £20,718. This figure included a 50 foot turntable for the shed, which was supplied by Messrs. Cowans & Sheldon. Hellifield lost its passenger junction status in September 1962 when the line to Chatburn and Blackburn was closed to passengers, and it suffered a further blow when the engine shed was shut in June 1963. The remote location of the locomotive shed resulted in its selection as a storage shed for stock preserved in the National Collection, but when it was no longer needed for this purpose it was demolished. This fate could have overtaken the bleak and windswept station buildings, had it not been for the vigilance of the local authority. *Brian Magilton*

Photographed near Settle Junction in superb low winter lighting conditions, BR Standard Class 9F No.92012 attacks the first few yards of the 'Long Drag' with a short train of empty hoppers from Widnes to Long Meg sidings, near Lazonby, on 13th February 1965. The tracks of the line to Lancaster, from which a line diverged at Clapham to Ingleton, are visible in the foreground. The line from Skipton to Ingleton was the first railway route in this area, and was opened by the North Western Railway in 1849. At Ingleton a direct connection was built in 1861 by the London & North Western Railway (LNWR) to Low Gill on the West Coast Main Line. The line through Ingleton was, however, closed to passengers in 1954, and to freight from 1st March 1965. It was dismantled shortly afterwards, despite being a useful diversionary route when the Settle & Carlisle line was blocked by a mishap. Trains on the Lancaster line were diverted to run via Carnforth following closure of the Wennington to Lancaster (Green Ayre) section from 3rd January 1966. Settle Junction was once the site of an interchange station between North Western Railway and Settle & Carlisle trains.

Alan Robey

The beginning of the long climb – mainly at 1 in 100 – to Blea Moor can be clearly seen, as the train depicted in the previous picture passes the photographer, with a clear road ahead. Settle station was located over a mile further on, beyond the deep cutting which is just discernible in the distance. In November 1869, the start of construction work on the Settle & Carlisle line was marked by a ceremony at Anley, between Settle Junction and Settle station, when the first sod was cut.

Alan Robey

BR Standard 'Britannia' Pacific No.70029 *Shooting Star*, which is in quite clean external conditon, crosses the A65 main road at Settle on 18th April 1967. The Pacific was working the 12.55pm Stourton to Carlisle freight, a regular 'Britannia' working at that time. This was a rather humble duty for No.70029, which was built in 1952, and spent the first part of its career at Cardiff Canton shed, on the Western Region, powering crack expresses from South Wales to Paddington. *Shooting Star* was withdrawn from service six months after this photograph was taken. *Gavin Morrison*

Railway photographers have complained endlessly about the sun's unfortunate habit of disappearing behind a tiny cloud just as a 'master shot' of a passing train was about to be taken. On this occasion, however, the sun appears to have burst through a sombre sky just at the right moment after a heavy shower, producing a brilliant lighting effect. For once, luck was on the photographer's side! Here, LMSR Class 6P5F 'Jubilee' No.45647 *Sturdee* makes a stirring sight, just north of Settle, at the head of a relief 'Thames-Clyde Express' on 23rd March 1967. Sadly, No.45647 was withdrawn from service a month after this picture was taken, after it failed a boiler test, so this may have been its swan song on main line passenger work.   *Peter Fitton*

The 3.40pm Bradford Forster Square to Carlisle stopping train is seen north of Settle with 'Royal Scot' No.46152 *The King's Dragoon Guardsman* in charge, on 3rd April 1965. Despite the locomotive's presentable external condition, this is understood to have been No.46152's final run, it being withdrawn from traffic a few days afterwards. No.46152 is believed to have been originally built in 1927 by the North British Locomotive Co. as No.6100 *Royal Scot*. In 1933 Nos 6100 and 6152 changed their identities, and the original No.6152 became No.6100. This was undertaken in connection with the 'Century of Progress' exhibition in North America, for which the LMSR sent 'No.6100' and a rake of carriages. The train's unusual formation will be noted; two of the three passenger vehicles on the rear appear to be just ex-works, and apparently include a Derby Lightweight diesel multiple unit, which was presumably *en route* to Carlisle as empty stock for use on local services.

Peter Fitton

The Railway Correspondence & Travel Society arranged a 'Rebuilt Scot Commemorative' railtour for 13th February 1965, using No.46160 *Queen Victoria's Rifleman*. Unfortunately, No.46160 failed with a hot axlebox a week before the tour, so No.46115 *Scots Guardsman* had to be hastily prepared instead. In the space of a few days Crewe North shed transformed a grubby, nameless locomotive into a fitting example of the class in its heyday. A set of false nameplates, made of plywood, were manufactured by a joiner to complete the effect. The special was routed from Crewe via Boars Head Junction over the Lancashire Union line from Chorley to Blackburn, a 'Black Five' pilot being assigned over this steeply graded stretch. The former shed at Hellifield, which by that time was being used to house historical relics preserved as part of the National Collection, was especially opened for the participants. Later, on the return run from Carlisle to Crewe via the West Coast route, the 'Royal Scot' gave a good account of itself, covering the Penrith to Shap Summit section in just over seventeen minutes. In this portrait, No.46115 is seen crossing Sheriff Brow Viaduct at Stainforth. *Scots Guardsman* survived in service until December 1965, by which time it had become the last active example of its class, and was subsequently bought for preservation.

Alan Robey

The year 1967 was one which saw the rapid elimination of steam traction from many areas of Great Britain, and by the end of that year steam power was confined to its last refuge in the north west of England. The weekend of 30th September/1st October saw the virtual withdrawal of steam in the West Riding of Yorkshire, and the closure of most of the area's last steam sheds. On September 30th, Holbeck shed marked the end of steam by turning out its last two remaining 'Jubilee' Class 4-6-0s: No.45593 *Kolhapur* worked the 2.40pm Leeds to Heysham parcels train, while sister engine No.45562 *Alberta* powered the 1.30pm Hunslet to Carlisle freight. *Alberta*, emitting a towering smoke effect, is depicted climbing through the Stainforth Gorge *en route* to Carlisle. In addition to its usual payload, the train also conveyed a brake van carrying members of the Railway Correspondence & Travel Society's West Riding branch. The crew of No.45562 had evidently resolved that the 'Jubilee' would go out in a blaze of glory, and the train reportedly sped past Settle Junction at 60mph. This effort apparently winded *Alberta* however, and speed had fallen to 12mph by the time Helwith Bridge was reached. From there on slow but steady progress was made up the 'Long Drag' to Blea Moor.

Jim Winkley

Judging by the numerous enthusiasts' heads leaning out of the windows, not to mention the sparkling condition of the locomotive, this train has the misleading appearance of a railtour. It is actually an ordinary Settle & Carlisle line passenger working, and was photographed at Stainforth during the summer of 1967. The motive power is No.45562 *Alberta*, which is hauling a northbound relief on an unknown date.

Derek Huntriss

Class 6P5F 'Jubilee' No.45562 *Alberta* plods past Helwith Bridge with the 1.30pm Hunslet to Carlisle freight on 30th September 1967. At this point the railway leaves the gorge of the River Ribble and enters the much more open valley of Upper Ribblesdale. The ruling gradient up the 'Long Drag' from Settle Junction to Blea Moor is 1 in 100, but north of Helwith Bridge there is a short level section where the line crosses the site of an old glacial lake. This no doubt gave hard-pressed firemen a brief respite during the long climb to the summit. There were two sets of sidings at Helwith Bridge, serving the Helwith Bridge Granite Company and the Ribblesdale Lime Works. Both were taken out of use on 7th September 1969, from which date Helwith Bridge signal box was closed.

Derek Huntriss

An unidentified LMSR 'Class Five' toils upgrade between Helwith Bridge and Horton-in-Ribblesdale with a long freight train in tow, an everyday scene that must have been repeated many times over the years. The open and exposed countryside on this section of the line is in marked contrast to the stretch between Settle and Helwith Bridge, where the line is hemmed in on both sides.

Derek Huntriss

Right, above: In addition to traversing wonderful countryside where steam engines could be photographed working to their limit, the Settle & Carlisle line was also justly famed for its attractive stations, which blended perfectly with the landscape. Many of these were beautifully decorated, as seen here at Horton-in-Ribblesdale station on 17th August 1958. 'All Ways Lead to the Delightful Dales', proclaims the sign on the up platform, which lists ornithology, caving, geology and walking as some of the pastimes for which the area was famous. Behind the fence, the station house is visible, while the background is dominated by the brooding presence of Pen-y-Ghent, one of the three peaks of this area.

Neil Thexton

Right, below: Horton-in-Ribblesdale station – located at an altitude of 850ft – boasted some of the most beautiful station gardens on the Settle & Carlisle line, as seen here, also on 17th August 1958. The excellence of the station's floral displays was officially recognised when it won the 'Best Kept Garden' competition for seventeen years in succession. In addition, the station also won many awards for its cleanliness and tidiness. There was a large lime works at Horton-in-Ribblesdale, which was served by sidings south of the station, and generated much business for the railway.

Neil Thexton

During the summer of 1967 the Settle & Carlisle line was invaded by hoards of photographers who came to record the exploits of the last 'Jubilee' 6P5F Class 4-6-0s. The most impressive workings on the line at that time, however, were probably the very heavy trains of concrete sleeper track panels, which generally ran from Dewsnap, near Guide Bridge, Manchester, to Carlisle on a Saturday afternoon. In this shot a pair of begrimed BR Standard Class 9Fs, Nos 92125 and 92071, are seen struggling up the 1 in 100 gradient north of Horton-in-Ribblesdale on 5th August 1967. The photographer was fortunate that the sun broke through the clouds just at the right time, on what appears to have been a very blustery day, with a strong westerly wind.   *Peter Fitton*

The Settle & Carlisle line often experiences atrocious weather conditions, with high winds accompanied by horizontal rain, and at times of bad weather it is difficult to imagine a more inhospitable region in Great Britain than the Pennines. A particularly appalling day, which will be long remembered by many steam enthusiasts, was 4th June 1966, when the Locomotive Club of Great Britain ran a railtour from London over the line. It was raining when the train left Carlisle, and by the time the more scenic sections of the line had been reached, the weather conditions had become so bad that the fells were almost totally obscured by low cloud and mist, which must have been a huge disappointment to travellers on the train. Despite the inclement conditions, the train paused for a photographic stop at Ribblehead, and Class 6P5F 'Jubilee' Nos. 45593 *Kolhapur* and 45596 *Bahamas* are seen waiting in pouring rain. The unlucky participants had further cause for complaint later in the journey when their train was delayed by damage to the overhead wires, south of Crewe.

Hugh Ballantyne

LMSR designed Class 5MT No.44767 coasts downhill through Ribblehead station with a southbound freight in tow on 21st September 1966. The unmistakable outline of Whernside provides a superb backdrop. Like some other stations on the Settle & Carlisle line, Ribblehead became a focal point for the local community, and for some years, until the mid-1950s, church services were held in the booking hall each Sunday. No.44767 was unique among the 842 'Black Five' locomotives. It was built at Crewe Works in 1947, and was equipped with outside Stephenson link motion, Timken roller bearings and a double chimney, as well as electric lighting. The double chimney did not last for long however, being removed in 1953. The engine was shedded at Bank Hall depot, Liverpool, and was a regular sight on trans-Pennine passenger workings from Liverpool to Leeds, via the Calder Valley line. It also spent a period based at Southport shed, presumably for working Manchester trains. During the twilight of its BR career No.44767 was based at Carlisle (Kingmoor) and became a familiar sight along the Settle & Carlisle line, usually on freight duties to the West Riding. It survived in service until Kingmoor shed was closed in December 1967, but happily was preserved, and can sometimes be seen in action on main line specials.

Peter Fitton

'A journey into the unknown' might well be an appropriate description of this picture of Class 8F No.48537 pounding through Ribblehead station with a down freight on 3rd April 1966. On a clear day the slopes of Whernside would be visible from this spot, but on this occasion visibility was considerably impaired by swirling mist, and Whernside, 2,419 feet above sea level, was almost totally hidden from view. Initially, the MR could not decide on a name for the station at this location, and it was often referred to as 'Ingleton Road' or 'Batty Green'. Ribblehead was eventually decided upon following a suggestion from a minister in Settle. No.48537 was one of a small batch of Class 8Fs built at Doncaster, and emerged from the works in July 1945 and was on loan to the LNER until 1947. It remained in service until October 1967.

Brian Magilton

On a lovely spring day in April 1966, Class 8F 2-8-0 No.48093 plods up the final couple of miles or so of the 'Long Drag', from Ribblehead station to the summit, which is beyond Blea Moor signal box. The train is made up of traditional short wheelbase, possibly unbraked, freight vehicles, which are no longer seen on the national system, and were being phased out even at the time of this photograph. Ribblehead station, which is 12½ miles from Settle Junction, and stands at a height of 1,025 feet, is in a particularly exposed position. Sometimes the westerly wind has been strong enough to tear the wagon sheets off trains crossing the viaduct, and Ribblehead can also experience exceptionally heavy rainfall, the annual average being about 70 inches. In 1938 the authorities recognised Ribblehead's harsh climatic conditions when it became an official meteorological reporting point, and in addition to his normal duties the station master made hourly daytime reports to the Air Ministry. During 1954 an incredible 109½ inches of rainfall was recorded. No.48093 was constructed as LMSR No.8093 by Vulcan Foundry, Newton-le-Willows, Lancashire, in 1937 and was requisitioned for military service in 1941, becoming War Department No.70621. In June 1943 it returned to LMSR service, regaining its original running number, and subsequently survived in traffic until it was withdrawn in November 1967.

Brian Magilton

Right, above: During construction of the Settle & Carlisle line in the 1870s, numerous navvy encampments were set up along the route. One of the largest was at Batty Green, immediately north-east of Ribblehead station, where a hutted township was built on the bare moorland, in one of the wildest and most remote locations on the entire line. The settlement consisted of living huts made of stone or rough timber, and roofed with felt. In addition to the huts, the encampment had a school, post office, library and a mission house. A hospital was constructed in 1871 following an outbreak of smallpox. The primitive living conditions, combined with the harsh climate, plus the extremely hard and dangerous work, resulted in many deaths amongst the workforce, which numbered 2,000 men at its peak. More than 100 navvies were laid to rest in the graveyard at St. Leonards Church, Chapel-le-Dale, between Ribblehead and Ingleton, which is depicted in this photograph taken on 29th September 1967.
Neville Simms

Right, below: A marble plaque was erected in the church at Chapel-le-Dale to commemorate those who lost their lives during construction of the line. The plaque was installed at the joint expense of the MR and the workmen who toiled, in intolerable conditions, for many years to complete construction of railway works around Ribblehead.
Neville Simms

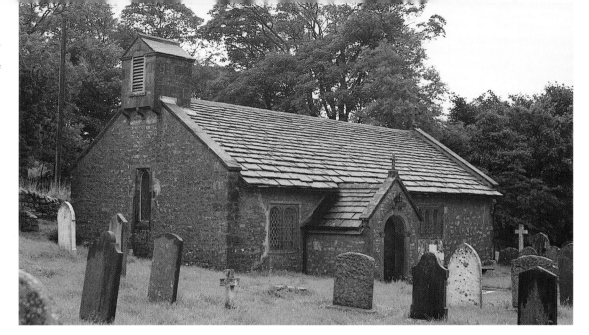

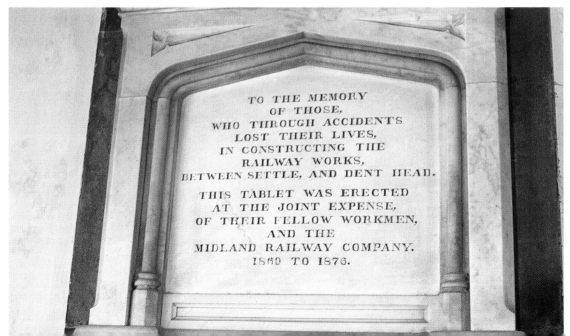

TO THE MEMORY
OF THOSE,
WHO THROUGH ACCIDENTS
LOST THEIR LIVES,
IN CONSTRUCTING THE
RAILWAY WORKS,
BETWEEN SETTLE, AND DENT HEAD.

THIS TABLET WAS ERECTED
AT THE JOINT EXPENSE,
OF THEIR FELLOW WORKMEN,
AND THE
MIDLAND RAILWAY COMPANY.
1869 TO 1876.

The 1.30pm Hunslet to Carlisle freight crosses Ribblehead Viaduct behind converted Crosti-boilered Class 9F 2-10-0 No.92021 on 5th August 1967. Ribblehead Viaduct (or Batty Moss Viaduct, as it is sometimes called) is undoubtedly the best-known and most impressive structure on the Settle & Carlisle line. The viaduct, which is 440 yards in length and 104 feet high, consists of twenty-four arches, every sixth, or 'king' pier, being specially strengthened. The first stone was laid on 12th October 1870 and by the end of 1873 the contractor's locomotives were able to cross the viaduct, which was completed in 1875. The stone used in its construction was quarried between Selside and Ribblehead. Over the years the viaduct has withstood the fiercest Pennine wind and the most violent storms. It bears ample testament to the skill of the Victorian engineers who designed the structure, and the endurance of the navvies who worked in appalling conditions to build this remarkable feat of engineering.

Roger Cruse

The 9.20am St. Pancras to Glasgow train – the relief 'Thames Clyde Express' – traverses the bare moorland between Ribblehead and Blea Moor behind 'Jubilee' 4-6-0 No.45593 *Kolhapur* on 5th August 1967. The train has almost reached the summit of the line, which is located just inside Blea Moor Tunnel, so the arduous fifteen mile climb from Settle Junction is almost over for No.45593's crew, who will now be able to take it relatively easy for the remainder of the journey to Carlisle. The year 1967 was a sad one for steam enthusiasts, who experienced the swift elimination of steam traction from many parts of Great Britain. The regular use of 6P5F Class 'Jubilees' on summer Saturday express workings over the Settle & Carlisle line, on which they had worked for thirty years, was one of the highlights of the year, and gave considerable pleasure to many steam fans. *Roger Cruse*

The splendour of the Settle & Carlisle line is superbly captured in this early morning photograph of Class 6P5F 'Jubilee' No.45697 *Achilles* climbing towards Blea Moor with a northbound freight on 13th June 1966. The backdrop is provided by Whernside, its summit shrouded in a thin layer of cloud, on what appears to be a perfect morning. No.45697 was constructed at Crewe Works in April 1936, and survived to become one of the last three active 'Jubilees'. It was withdrawn from service in September 1967.

Roy Hobbs

Ten BR Standard Class 6P5F 'Clan' Pacifics were constructed, the first example emerging from Crewe Works in December 1951, and they were evenly divided between Carlisle (Kingmoor) and Glasgow (Polmadie) sheds. There were plans to construct a further fifteen members of the class, and the names of the additional engines had already been selected when the order for those engines was cancelled. The 'Clans' were only moderately powered for their size, and often criticised for poor steaming, a characteristic that did not endear them to locomotive crews. In service, the Scottish-based engines could often be found on the Glasgow to Liverpool/Manchester trains, while the Carlisle locomotives regularly worked to Glasgow, Aberdeen and Stranraer, in addition to other duties. Withdrawals commenced in December 1962 when the entire Scottish

Region allocation was condemned *en masse*, at a time when BR was engaged in an orgy of destruction of steam power – apparently for accountancy purposes – just prior to the creation of the British Railways Board. The engines based at Carlisle survived for much longer however, and were not withdrawn until due for heavy repairs. By the mid-1960s the survivors were frequently rostered for secondary duties, such as that seen in this picture of No.72006 *Clan Mackenzie* hauling an up local train near Blea Moor on 15th May 1965. At the time of this photograph, there were still four 'Clans' in traffic, but they were gradually withdrawn and No.72006 became the final survivor. It was eventually condemned in May 1966 and subsequently broken up in J. McWilliam's yard at Shettleston, outside Glasgow.

R.K. Greenhalgh/Colour-Rail

Of all the locomotive classes that were regular performers on the Settle & Carlisle line during the closing years of steam, it was pictures of Class 6P5F Hughes/Fowler 'Crab' 2-6-0s that proved amongst the most elusive. In this view No.42793 is seen beginning the long descent from Blea Moor to Settle Junction with a southbound freight in tow, sometime in the early 1960s. The first 'Crab' made its appearance in 1926 and eventually a total of 245 engines was constructed. No.42793 was built as LMSR No.13093 at Crewe in October 1927, and was renumbered to 2793 in the mid-1930s. It lasted in traffic until December 1964. The 'Crabs' were popular locomotives with enginemen, being good steamers, sure-footed and strong on the banks, all valuable qualities on such a demanding line as the Settle & Carlisle! Loop lines, which are partially visible in the picture, were installed at Blea Moor in 1941 as a wartime measure. In April 1952, Blea Moor was the site of a potentially serious accident when a loose brake rod on the tender of a Compound 4-4-0 came adrift when it was piloting a 'Royal Scot' at the head of the up 'Thames Clyde Express'. The brake rod became entangled with pointwork, causing the blades to move beneath No.46117 *Welsh Guardsman*, which toppled onto its side, together with five coaches. Fortunately, the train was travelling slowly at the time and no passengers were seriously hurt.

Colour-Rail

Despite steam traction being ousted from the regular expresses in 1961, it still remained possible to experience steam travel over the Settle & Carlisle line on a stopping train, until diesel units took over in April 1966. Two local trains were provided in each direction on weekdays between Hellifield and Carlisle, one of which in each direction also served stations to or from Bradford Forster Square. In addition, there was an early morning working from Appleby to Carlisle, and an evening return train. There was also an early morning train from Garsdale to Hellifield which was formed of a supposedly empty train from Skipton. Sometimes, and certainly during the last summer of steam on the line, the 'empty' working often conveyed steam photographers, and was better patronised than the train it later formed! Latterly, the local services were powered by 'Black Fives' or 'Britannias', but 'Clan' Pacifics, some of which were based at Carlisle (Kingmoor) shed, also appeared. Here, on a bright morning in April 1966, a Hellifield to Carlisle 'all stations' train, hauled by 'Britannia' Pacific No.70006 *Robert Burns* is seen in the delightful surroundings of Dentdale. *Brian Magilton*

The 6.40am SO Birmingham to Glasgow train, hauled by Class 6P5F No.45593 *Kolhapur*, emerges from Blea Moor Tunnel on a sunny 22nd July 1967. Though not as immediately impressive as the many splendid viaducts on the Settle & Carlisle line, the construction of Blea Moor Tunnel was, perhaps, the greatest engineering achievement of all. The 2,629 yards long tunnel was built between 1870 and 1875 at a cost of £45 a yard and the principal explosive used in its construction was dynamite, which was imported by the MR at a cost of £200 per ton. The long suffering navvies had to work by candlelight, for which the MR had to foot a bill of £50 per month, and the temperature underground sometimes reached 80°F. Tunnelling work proceeded from sixteen faces using seven shafts sunk from the top of the moor which, in some places, is 500 feet above track level. Three of the shafts used in the construction of the tunnel were later retained for ventilation purposes. In the author's opinion, one of the highlights of a journey along the line occurs when the train bursts out of the dank and noisy cavern of Blea Moor Tunnel, and into the beautiful landscape of Dentdale.

Peter Fitton

A pair of unidentified Class 8Fs trundle across Dent Head Viaduct with a train of concrete sleeper track, sometime during the summer of 1967. The route of the railway as it hugs the slopes of Widdale Fell, in the background on the right, can be clearly discerned, and the cluster of buildings around Dent station can just be seen. *Derek Huntriss*

An unidentified up express, hauled by LMSR Class 7P 'Patriot' 4-6-0 No.45521 *Rhyl* traverses Shale Cutting, between Dent Head and Arten Gill viaducts, on 5th August 1961. The train is riding high above the bottom of the dale, which is out of sight on the left of the shot. Shale Cutting is particularly vulnerable to blockage by snow in the winter, but at least it is not so susceptible to flooding!

When the line was built the MR wisely constructed an aqueduct, visible in the background, which was designed to carry water from Wold Fell across the railway. No doubt it has prevented flooding of the line on many occasions over the years, when an especially violent storm has broken over the fells.

Graham Hoare

LMSR Class 6P5F 'Crab' 2-6-0 No.42876 enters Shale Cutting with a southbound freight on 5th August 1961. Universally known as 'Crabs' due to their high running plate and rather ungainly appearance, these machines were a familiar sight on the Settle & Carlisle line for many years, though they do not appear to have been widely photographed in colour. The last remaining 'Crabs' were withdrawn from BR service in early 1967.   *Graham Hoare*

Arten Gill Viaduct carries the railway across Arten Gill beck, which tumbles down a gap in the side of the valley which was cut by a post-glacial stream. It is one of the best known, and arguably the most graceful, of all of the structures on the Settle & Carlisle line. The 220 yards long, eleven arch viaduct was built entirely of local stone, known as Dent marble, which is a dark grey limestone with white fossils. Construction of Arten Gill Viaduct started on 3rd May 1871 and took four years to complete. Some piers had to be sunk as much as fifty-five feet below ground level until a firm foundation was secured. Here, BR Standard Class 7P6F 'Britannia' Pacific No.70016 *Ariel* races across the viaduct with the 9.20am SO St. Pancras to Glasgow, the relief 'Thames Clyde Express', on 22nd July 1967.

Peter Fitton

On the beautiful summer's evening of 5th June 1966 WD Class 2-8-0 No.90243, in charge of a northbound freight, lays a smoke screen across the fells as it swings around the curve at the approach to Dent station. Arten Gill Viaduct is prominent in the background. Note also the remnants of the snow fences on the hillside, which were built to prevent snowdrifts on the line. No.90243, which was built by the North British Locomotive Co., Glasgow (works No.25200), was originally WD No.77332 and came into BR ownership in 1949, working at first on the Western Region. The locomotive spent the greater part of its BR career based in the West Riding however, and saw service mainly at Wakefield and Royston sheds, presumably employed on coal trains, so perhaps it was something of a rarity on the Settle & Carlisle line. It was withdrawn from traffic at Normanton shed in May 1967.   *A.E.R. Cope/Colour-Rail*

In 1960, when a batch of Gresley Class A3 Pacifics was allocated to Holbeck shed, Leeds, the reaction amongst the shed staff and enginemen is likely to have been one of total surprise and disbelief. The shed had a long LMSR tradition, where the engine crews had been brought up on rebuilt 'Royal Scots' and 'Jubilees', so the allocation of A3s was a very radical and unexpected step. Many of the A3s were not, so to speak, in 'A1' condition, but despite this the local crews took to them, and particularly appreciated their free steaming capabilities and comfortable cabs. By November 1960 nine A3s were on the books at Holbeck, principally for use on the Scottish expresses north of Leeds,

and it is unlikely that Holbeck had previously seen such a sizeable complement of powerful engines. In addition to its own allocation, Holbeck frequently borrowed examples from Neville Hill shed, these being in rather better mechanical condition than its own locomotives. One of these, No.60074 *Harvester,* is seen heading the down 'Thames Clyde Express' at Dent on 8th April 1961. Sadly, the reign of the A3s was destined to be very short lived, because they were largely ousted by diesels a few months later.

Gavin Morrison

Between 19th and 24th January 1963 the Settle & Carlisle line was completely blocked by some of the worst snowdrifts in living memory. In the early hours of 20th January the 10.5pm (previous day) Edinburgh to St. Pancras sleeping car train encountered deep snowdrifts near Dent and was forced to return to Carlisle, from where it proceeded to London via Newcastle. Midland Line expresses were diverted over Shap and then along the Low Gill to Clapham line, from where they reached their normal route at Settle Junction. The usual motive power arrangements were disrupted, and diverted services produced some remarkable and probably unprecedented sights, such as a 'Princess Coronation' Pacific on the up 'Waverley' on 23rd January and V2 Class No.60802 on the southbound 'Thames Clyde Express' on the following day. Here, a northbound freight with 'Black Five' No 45491 in charge, is depicted passing through Dent station on 26th January shortly after the line re-opened. The line was blocked again by snow during the following month and normal services were not totally resumed for some weeks afterwards. Perhaps the most incredible thing about this shot is that the photographer was able to reach this icy, snowbound location to take the picture! *Gavin Morrison*

LMSR-designed Class 8F No.48743 trundles through Dent station with a northbound freight in August 1966. Dent station, which is 1,150 feet above sea level and the highest main line station in England, is superbly situated on a ledge on the side of Widdale Fell, overlooking Dentdale. It is approached by an incredibly steep zig-zag road, which climbs up from the hamlet of Cowgill, which is on the valley floor hundreds of feet below. In bygone days this road, which continues across the moors to Garsdale station, served some now-closed coal pits on the slopes of Widdale Fell, and was known locally as the 'coal road'. The MR could not decide on the site for Dent station, and various places were considered – including such unlikely locations as Dent Head and Arten Gill – before the existing site was agreed. This indecision caused a delay in building the station, which was eventually opened in 1877. At one time the MR were presented with a petition by the inhabitants of Dent village who, no doubt disappointed that their settlement was to be so remote from the station, put forward a proposal for a branch to be built from the main line! No.48743 is an interesting machine. It was built at Darlington Works in 1946 and initially ran as LNER Class O6 No.3138, being renumbered 3538 during the following year. In October 1947 it was transferred to LMSR ownership, and therefore just obtained its LMSR number (8743) before nationalisation! *Brian Magilton*

A southbound freight, headed by 'Black Five' No.44727, passes over Garsdale troughs on 22nd July 1967. One or two moorland cottages are just visible down in the valley and give some idea of the location of the railway at this point, which is perched on a ledge on the fell side. No.44727 is no ordinary 'Black Five', because it was one of a small batch of ten locomotives built with steel instead of copper fireboxes. It was constructed at Crewe Works in March 1949 and remained in traffic until October 1967. *Roger Cruse*

Photographed in absolutely diabolical weather conditions, for which the Settle & Carlisle line has an unenviable reputation, LMSR 'Jubilee' No.45562 *Alberta*, working a northbound passenger train, is seen taking water on Garsdale troughs in August 1967. The train is approaching Garsdale's splendid wooden down distant signal. The water troughs at Garsdale, the highest in Great Britain, were installed in 1907. They are 1,670 feet long and hold between five and six thousand gallons of water, of which up to two thousand gallons at a time can be taken by a locomotive's tender. On a clear day there is a magnificent view from this vantage point, but on the day of this photograph the scene was almost completely obscured by mist and driving rain.

Derek Huntriss

An up stopping train, probably the 4.37pm from Carlisle to Bradford Forster Square, pauses at Garsdale behind a BR Standard 'Britannia' Pacific No.70035 *Rudyard Kipling*, sometime in August 1964. Haulage of this three-coach local train could hardly have been the high point of No.70035's career, but at least the engine was still in revenue-earning service! The locomotive was in a filthy condition, but was still carrying its nameplates. The train waits the 'right away' in glorious, golden evening sunshine, and is seen against a sombre background of dark storm clouds. Perhaps the sun appeared at just the right time for the photographer, which does sometimes happen, even on the Settle & Carlisle line! Note the gentleman sitting in the engine's cab, who was presumably an enthusiast enjoying the rare treat of an unofficial footplate ride.

A.E.R. Cope/Colour-Rail

Garsdale was the only true junction station on the Settle & Carlisle line and has an absorbing history. The station was originally known as Hawes Junction, and has had other names over the years, the present name dating from 1932. Besides being the junction for the Hawes branch, during the halcyon days of the MR Garsdale station was a busy place, being the point at which pilot engines were detached from most trains, and it was not unusual for the signalman to have half a dozen light engines on his hands, all waiting to return to Carlisle or Hellifield. The MR had grandiose plans for a large engine shed at Garsdale, but ran out of funds. A shed was eventually constructed by the NER, but this closed in 1939. In addition to providing the few local inhabitants with a valuable rail link, for many years the station doubled as a community centre. Church services were held in the waiting room, which also served as a library. There was a stage beneath the water tank, together with a piano and upholstered chairs where the 'locals' could get together for their social life. This photograph was taken on 12th July 1964 and the view is looking north towards Carlisle.

Alan Robey

Right, above: Judging by the good weather conditions seen in this view, the Railway Correspondence & Travel Society certainly selected a pleasant day for the start of their five days long 'North Eastern Railtour', which is depicted during a photographic stop at Garsdale on 27th September 1963. The bright sunshine beautifully illuminates a fine array of MR signals and dapples the fells beyond in this photograph, which was apparently taken from the signal box's verandah. Note also the track of the Hawes branch, which is on the extreme right hand side adjacent to the cutting. Some society members, soberly dressed by today's standards, congregate around the engine, No.46238 *City of Carlisle*, in the hope of obtaining a shot before the train moves off, or the sun disappears. An up freight train, hauled by a Class 4F 0-6-0, passed through Garsdale during the railtour's stop but, alas, the sun was hidden by a cloud at the wrong moment, and an interesting shot was ruined. *J. Spencer Gilks*

Right, below: Garsdale was, as previously stated, the station at which pilot locomotives were detached from both northbound and southbound trains in bygone days. The MR's plans for an engine shed at Garsdale may not have materialised, but at least a turntable was installed, presumably so that engine crews were not forced to return home tender first in bad weather conditions. There is a remarkable tale of an engine being turned on a wild night when it was caught broadside by a severe wind, and according to several accounts continued spinning like a merry-go-round for some hours afterwards. In order to prevent a repetition, the turntable was later surrounded by a stockade constructed from old sleepers. When piloting declined, the turntable was used less frequently, but North Eastern Region-based locomotives working into Garsdale continued to turn there regularly until the closure of the line from Hawes to Northallerton in April 1954. In this extremely rare picture of the stockaded turntable, a D20 Class 4-4-0, No.62347, is seen being turned in October 1953. This class of sixty locomotives was originally introduced by Wilson Worsdell, the North Eastern Railway's Chief Engineer, between 1899 and 1907. The last survivor was withdrawn in 1957. *I. Davidson/Colour-Rail*

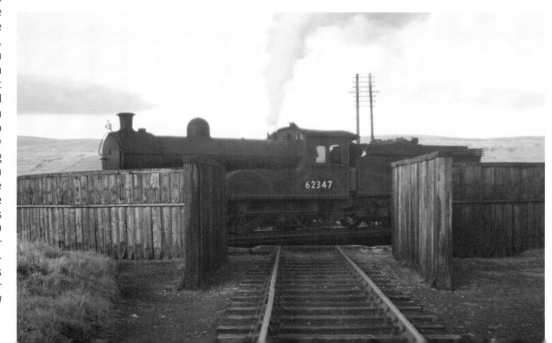

The branch line from Garsdale to Hawes was authorised by Parliament as part of the original Act sanctioning the Settle & Carlisle line. Work on the Hawes branch was deferred until most of the main line had been completed, and was further delayed as a result of an exceptionally wet winter in 1877/78; it eventually opened on 1st October 1878. The Hawes branch had three notable engineering works, Mossdale Head Tunnel (245 yards), Appersett Viaduct and Mossdale Gill Viaduct. There was a joint station with the North Eastern Railway at Hawes, from where the NER operated trains down Wensleydale to Northallerton. After World War Two, traffic on this line declined sharply and passenger services were withdrawn from 26th April 1954, though much of the route remained open for many years afterwards to serve a quarry at Redmire. The section from Garsdale to Hawes survived for a further five years, closing on 16th March 1959. During this period, a meagre service of one train in each direction ran daily, primarily for the benefit of railwaymen who worked on the Settle & Carlisle line. In this picture, Stanier Class 4MT 2-6-4T No.42484 is seen against a background of bleak moorland scenery near Mossdale Head on 7th March 1959 just over a week prior to the withdrawal of the service.

Neil Thexton

An interesting picture of Hawes station taken on 7th March 1959, during the last days of passenger services. No.42484, which is seen in the previous picture, is presumably about to run around its coaches before forming the 4.25pm to Hellifield, which by this time was the only outward passenger train of the day. Note that there are a number of freight vehicles in the goods yard. Hawes retained goods facilities from Northallerton until 1964, long after the complete closure of the line to Garsdale. At first, Hawes had two signal boxes, Hawes East and Hawes West, but in 1900 they were replaced by a new signal box, which was located east of the station, and officially known as 'Hawes Station': this is just visible on the extreme left. The NER was apparently responsible for maintenance of all the signalling equipment and structures. Today, the station has found a new lease of life as a tourist information centre and the former goods yard has become, inevitably perhaps, a car park. In addition, an industrial steam locomotive, plus some BR Standard Mk.1 coaches, are (at the time of writing) statically preserved on the former station site.

Neil Thexton

A Skipton to Carlisle 'pick-up' goods train, hauled by 'Britannia' Pacific No.70028 *Royal Star*, crosses the Sedburgh to Hawes main road, north of Garsdale station, on 28th April 1967. No.70028 began life in October 1952 working from Cardiff (Canton) shed on the Western Region, but was displaced by diesels in the early 1960s and moved to Aston shed, Birmingham. It was later based at Crewe (North) depot, before being transferred to Carlisle (Kingmoor), from where it was withdrawn in September 1967. The delightful building in the foreground is a small chapel. The bridge, officially known as Moorcock Road Bridge, is worthy of note. It is a 39 1/2 feet wide skew arch, with massive wing walls. This all-stone bridge, which like nearly all structures on the Settle & Carlisle line blends in very well with its surroundings, was built in 1872.

The late Derek Cross

Class 8F 2-8-0 No.48077 takes a northbound freight across Lunds Viaduct, the parapets of which are visible towards the rear of the train. The northern portal of Moorcock Tunnel can be seen in the background. No.8077 was built by Vulcan Foundry in December 1936, and was requisitioned by the government for military service in 1941 becoming War Department No.70611. It returned to everyday service in December 1949 and remained in use virtually until the end of BR steam, not being withdrawn until March 1968. This portrait was taken in September 1967.

J. Spencer Gilks

This photograph of LMSR Class 8F No.48090 leaving Shotlock Hill Tunnel with a Long Meg to Widnes anhydrite train has been published before and may be familiar to some readers. It is, however, one of the author's favourite Settle & Carlisle pictures because it was taken on 4th November 1967, the last full day that he spent on the line shortly before the demise of BR steam. It was the kind of day that railway photographers dream of, clear, cold and very frosty, and fortunately there was an early morning procession of northbound freight trains which made a superb spectacle in the splendid lighting conditions. It is likely that the crew of No.48090 will remember that day for altogether different reasons. Their locomotive was apparently in a parlous condition, and refused to steam on the long 1 in 100 climb from Kirkby Stephen to Ais Gill Summit. The laboured ascent occupied fifty minutes, but at least it gave chasing photographers a field day. A memorable occasion that will never be forgotten!

Gavin Morrison

The Ais Gill signalman gives the crew of Class 9F No.92056 a friendly wave as they surmount the summit with a Long Meg to Widnes freight train on 2nd June 1967. The small signal box must surely have been one of the most famous, and certainly one of the most isolated, in Great Britain. It was commissioned on 26th April 1890, and replaced an earlier box on the same site. For over ninety years it withstood the fierce Pennine storms which frequently rage in these parts, until it was taken out of use in January 1981, and later removed for preservation. Note the walkway from the rear of the box to the embankment. Ironically, despite being situated in one of the wettest parts of Great Britain, there was no running water at Ais Gill, and this vital commodity presumably had to be supplied daily by passing trains which were booked to stop for this purpose.

The late Derek Cross

Photographed on a dull and misty day, LMSR Class 4F No.44197 produces a memorable smoke effect as it breasts the summit at Ais Gill with a mixed southbound freight train on 15th September 1959. Despite being associated with the Settle & Carlisle line for a generation, colour pictures of these locomotives at work on the route are uncommon, so the author was delighted when this superb action shot was submitted. No.44197 was built in October 1925 at St. Rollox Works, Glasgow, and achieved almost forty years service, before being withdrawn in September 1964. No.44197 enjoyed the hospitality of Skipton shed for many years, and is thought to have been based there at the time of this picture, so it is likely that this train was a Carlisle to Skipton 'pick up' goods working.

Neil Thexton

The Class 9Fs were the most successful of the BR Standard designs, and it was particularly painful for steam enthusiasts to see the lives of these excellent locomotives cut short by rapid dieselisation in the 1960s. Like many other classes, some of the 9Fs were poorly maintained towards the end of steam, and here an engine in distress, No.92118, is depicted passing Ais Gill on a down freight in August 1967. Apart from the sadly neglected and badly leaking 9F, virtually everything else in this picture is perfect – a beautifully clear and bright morning, plus the breathtaking and unmistakable setting of Ais Gill, with its vast expanse of moorland stretching in all directions. *Derek Huntriss*

Right, above: The arduous climb to Ais Gill Summit was doubtless an ordeal for the footplate crews of engines that were shy of steam, and many enginemen must have been thankful and relieved when they finally reached the summit board. Here, one of the famous summit signs is seen on 12th July 1964, together with a quarter mile post which indicates the distance from St. Pancras.

Alan Robey

Right, below: Most steam railway photographers prefer pictures of locomotives emitting clouds of black smoke, which may enhance a photographic image, but is invariably a sign of inefficient combustion which is frequently caused by poor firing technique or poor quality coal! One wonders how many housewives, in times past, cursed the smoke from a passing train which ruined the Monday morning wash. Here, in this shot of Hughes/Fowler 'Crab' 2-6-0 No.42875 climbing to Ais Gill with a southbound freight, judging by the lack of exhaust the fireman appears to be doing his job expertly, as there is hardly a wisp of smoke to be seen. This photograph was taken on 13th May 1961.

Gavin Morrison

The 'Jubilees' were famous for their syncopated three-cylinder rhythm, and one can only imagine the tremendous sound being produced by No.45573 *Newfoundland* as it heaved its heavy load up the northern approach to Ais Gill. The train was a CTAC Scottish tours special from Gourock to Leicester, and this picture was taken on 17th July 1965. Despite the mighty effort being expended by the 'Jubilee', and its extremely neglected external condition, it appears to be coping admirably with its heavy train. No.45573 was destined to last for only a few more weeks after this picture was taken however, and was officially condemned in September 1965.   *Brian Magilton*

Colour photographs of LNER Class A3 Pacifics on the Settle & Carlisle line are extremely rare, so it is likely that this superb study of the up 'Thames Clyde Express', taken on 16th July 1960, is unique. The train engine is No.60038 *Firdaussi* which is piloted by 'Black Five' No.44896, and the location is, of course, the approach to Ais Gill. *Firdaussi* was one of the first members of its class to be based at Holbeck shed for workings over the Settle & Carlisle line,

arriving in February 1960. It remained at Holbeck, as the sole representative of its class, long after the other A3s had departed. During the winter of 1962/63 it spent a period in store, but emerged to work a variety of turns in the Leeds area, still based at Holbeck. It was eventually withdrawn from Neville Hill shed, Leeds, in November 1963.

Neil Thexton

A Stephenson Locomotive Society railtour, hauled by LMSR Class 8P 'Princess Coronation' Pacific No.46255, *City of Hereford*, nears Ais Gill Summit on 12th July 1964. No.46255 was built at Crewe Works in October 1946 during the last years of LMSR jurisdiction. Between August 1950 and April 1953 it ran in BR blue, and thereafter in green livery. During its twilight years No.46255 was employed on a variety of menial tasks on the West Coast Main Line, often working freight and van trains, in addition to powering seasonal dated passenger workings during the summer months. The Pacific also, no doubt, frequently deputised for failed diesels, but it was condemned in September 1964 when the LMR issued a sad decree that all the survivors of this celebrated class must be withdrawn from traffic. *Jim Winkley*

An LMSR Class 5MT 4-6-0 No.45027 plods steadily up the final few hundred yards to Ais Gill Summit with a southbound freight train on 12th August 1967, a typically dull and drizzly Pennine day. Notice that although the locomotive is working hard to keep its train on the move, there is hardly a trace of leaking steam at the front end, perhaps proving that at least some engines were being reasonably well maintained at this late stage in the run-down of BR steam. No.45027 was one of the oldest 'Black Fives' in traffic at this time, being a member of a batch of 100 engines built by Vulcan Foundry. It was built in September 1934 and lasted in service until May 1968. The permanent way hut, also seen in the picture, briefly rose to fame in the 1980s following its destruction by a lineside fire, which was apparently caused by sparks from a passing steam railtour. The local fire brigade attended, but were unable to save the hut which was well alight by the time they arrived at this isolated spot. According to the railway press, when the brigade submitted a report on the conflagration, BR allegedly stated that they had no record of any building at that location! *Derek Huntriss*

A very rare colour picture of a veteran MR Class 3F 0-6-0 on the Settle & Carlisle line. It is most unlikely that many pictures were taken in colour of these locomotives on the route. The engine, which appears to be No.43295, was photographed hauling a short goods train up to Ais Gill Summit on 8th November 1957, a crisp winter's day. What more need be said?

Neil Thexton

Photographed against the towering backdrop of Wild Boar Fell, which rises to 2,324 feet above sea level, a WD Class 2-8-0, No.90464, heads a freight train up to the summit on 15th September 1959. The train appears to be a block working, made up of hopper wagons of anhydrite, which was presumably *en route* from Long Meg sidings to Widnes. No.90464 was one of a number of these distinctive Austerity 2-8-0s built by Vulcan Foundry, this example emerging in 1944 as War Department No.78655. In 1946 it was purchased by the LNER, re-classified O7, and renumbered 3143. It would have become BR No.63143, but this number was never applied. In BR service No.90464 (as it later became) was initially based at Thornton Junction shed in Scotland, but later spent some time at St. Margarets shed, Edinburgh. Towards the end of its career No.90464 was based at Sutton Oak shed, near St. Helens, in Lancashire and was withdrawn from there in March 1964.

Neil Thexton

During the weekend of 4th/5th February 1967 a total of nine football specials ran from South Wales to Scotland in connection with a Scotland v. Wales Rugby Union International at Edinburgh. After the match the trains returned home from Edinburgh, diesel hauled by Brush Type 4s, over the Waverley route. From Carlisle the specials were routed over the Settle & Carlisle line, and 'Britannia' Pacifics were employed on five of these heavy trains which produced a memorable spectacle for photographers. In this shot, No. 70003 *John Bunyan* is depicted on the climb to Ais Gill with a train bound for Carmarthen. The location is Mallerstang Common, a remote spot where the railway is perched on a ledge high above the Moorcock to Kirkby Stephen road and the infant waters of the River Eden. *Peter Fitton*

Mallerstang signal box, seen here on the left of the picture, must have been the most inaccessible signal box on the Settle & Carlisle line, and was probably one of the most remote in Great Britain. The author could not, therefore, resist including this rare colour shot of No.45562 *Alberta* passing the box on 30th September 1967. The signal box was brought into use on 9th September 1894, on a site which had been earmarked for a passenger station in 1884. The latter project never got off the ground, due to insufficient local money being raised to finance construction of an approach road. The Garsdale to Kirkby Stephen section of the route therefore remained the longest stretch of line (9¾ miles) without a station. Up and down sidings were provided, in addition to a crossover between the main running lines. The original up and down starting signals were renewed in 1936 when tubular steel replaced the timber posts. The down distant was replaced by a colour light signal in 1952. The sidings were lifted in 1959 and the box was taken out of use on 31st August 1969. Towards the end, the signal box was only open at nightime, a busy period for freight traffic, and a night spent at this location, with a telephone as the only contact with the rest of civilisation, must have been quite an experience! In order to reach the box, the signalman would be faced with an uphill walk across fields from the nearest road, located half a mile away, hardly a prospect to relish on a wild Pennine night.

J. Spencer Gilks

LMSR Class 5MT No 45001 drifts down the 1 in 100 incline towards Kirkby Stephen with a Skipton to Carlisle 'pick up' freight on 2nd June 1967. No.45001 was a Crewe-built example, being outshopped in March 1935 and surviving in service until withdrawal came in March 1968. The 'Black Five' had clearly been smartened up shortly before this picture was taken, but the cleaners had apparently been unable to reach the top of the boiler. Mallerstang Common provides a splendid setting for this picture. The tiny cluster of buildings just visible in the distance, on the left of the picture, is the small hamlet of Outhgill.

The late Derek Cross

A welcome ray of sparkling, low winter sunshine beautifully illuminates this stirring shot of BR Standard Pacific No. 70039 *Sir Christopher Wren*, as it heads away from Kirkby Stephen, and on towards Ais Gill Summit, with a southbound special on 5th February 1967. This was another of the trains which was run in connection with the Scotland v. Wales Rugby Union International at Edinburgh, and in this case the passengers were returning to Swansea. Unfortunately, some of the locomotive's exhaust blew down in front of the camera, almost spoiling the picture, and a few wisps of steam are just visible in the foreground.

Peter Fitton

Hauling another of the returning Rugby Union football special trains bound for South Wales, 'Britannia' Pacific No.70010 *Owen Glendower* exerts maximum effort through Kirkby Stephen West station. This working was *en route* to Cardiff, so passengers had many hours of travelling ahead of them before they reached home. Kirkby Stephen has undergone a number of changes of name over the years, and in 1900 was renamed 'Kirkby Stephen and Ravenstonedale', a title which lasted until January 1935, when it reverted to its original name of Kirkby Stephen. In 1953 however, the suffix 'West' was added, when the former LNER station, on the Penrith to Darlington line, was renamed 'East'. Goods facilities were withdrawn from Kirkby Stephen West station in September 1964, and the station was (temporarily) closed to passenger traffic in May 1970. The station, which was some distance from the town it purported to serve, was the only one on the line to be constructed with a separate waiting room for first class passengers.

Peter Fitton

Class 5MT 4-6-0 No.44852, in charge of a southbound freight, was photographed from the end of Kirkby Stephen West station's down platform on 2nd June 1967. The train appears to be only modestly loaded, and hardly appears to be a taxing assignment for a 'Black Five'. The engine has just passed over the bridge which carries the railway across the main Kendal to Brough road, one of the few main roads the line encounters in the 72 miles between Settle Junction and Carlisle. No.44852 was constructed at Crewe Works in November 1944 and ran for only a further three months after this portrait was taken.

The late Derek Cross

A northbound freight, probably an empty anhydrite train from Widnes to Long Meg sidings, crosses Smardale Viaduct behind an unidentified BR Class 9F 2-10-0, sometime during the summer of 1966. This graceful, and magnificently situated twelve-arch structure, which was built entirely of grey limestone, is 237 yards long and 130 feet high. It is the tallest viaduct on the line, and took five years to build, being completed in June 1875. The viaduct carries the Settle & Carlisle line over Scandal beck, which is a tributary of the River Eden, but the beck is out of sight between the trees in the bottom of the picture. The viaduct also took the line over the former North Eastern Railway single track route from Tebay to Kirkby Stephen East, which passed beneath its most southerly arch. This line closed to regular traffic as long ago as 1st December 1952, but remained open for seasonal passenger workings until they also ceased at the end of the 1961 summer timetable.   *Derek Penney*

One of the great characteristics of the Settle & Carlisle line is the way in which so many of the original MR buildings have survived, almost untouched, since the day they were built. The fact that the MR never tackled anything half-heartedly, and built the structures so substantially in the first place, has no doubt assisted their longevity. In addition, the line's isolation probably discouraged any plans for the wholesale demolition of redundant buildings. There have been some regrettable exceptions to this rule however, notably the down platform at Ribblehead, which was demolished to make way for a stone terminal. Another loss was the impressive Appleby West signal box, which is seen here. The box was brought into use in 1890, and initially contained a 21 lever frame. From 1937 the box was known as 'Appleby Station', but was renamed 'Appleby West' in 1945, a name which it retained until closure occurred in October 1973. This picture was taken on 28th June 1964.

J. Spencer Gilks

A view of the south end of Appleby West station on 28th April 1967, showing LMSR Class 5MT 4-6-0 No.45236 taking water in the up platform. The 'Black Five' appears to be building up steam for the climb to Ais Gill which lay ahead. The main station buildings, with their decorative bargeboards, are just in the picture on the left, while the roof of the up side waiting room is also visible. Appleby station was the only one on the route to be deemed worthy of a passenger footbridge. This picture was taken from the extensive ten wagon cattle dock, the movement of livestock being a valuable source of income at Appleby. The Express Dairy Company's creamery, located south of the station, also brought business to the railway, the milk being regularly transported to London in tankers.

The late Derek Cross

Passengers were left in no doubt that they were at Appleby by this neat arrangement of stones behind the up platform, which was photographed on 28th June 1964. However, the standard BR 'sausage' sign shows 'Appleby West', the station name being changed from 'Appleby' in 1952 to avoid confusion with the nearby former North Eastern Railway station 'Appleby East', on the Penrith to Darlington line. Following the closure of the latter in 1962, the suffix 'West' was no longer necessary, and the station reverted to its original title in 1968.

J. Spencer Gilks

An Ivatt Class 4MT 2-6-0 No.43036 is pictured at Appleby West in this view, looking north, taken on 28th April 1967. The engine was working a local freight from Carlisle to Merrygill quarry, which was situated a few miles east of Kirkby Stephen, on the old NER route to Darlington via Stainmore. Part of this line, the embankment of which can be seen behind the trees on the right, was retained for freight only use following withdrawal of passenger services over the Stainmore route in 1962. There was a connection between the MR and NER routes at Appleby and this is clearly visible, just beyond the last vehicle of the train. Appleby North signal box can also be seen. This box which is of quite recent construction, dating from 1951, replaced an earlier structure, built in 1890, which was located just beyond the end of the down platform.

The late Derek Cross

A southbound freight, headed by a grimy Class 9F No.92110, strides across Long Marton Viaduct on 8th November 1967, as clouds scud across the top of the snow flecked Pennine Range in the background. The viaduct, which is 108 yards long and 60 feet high, was built mainly from red sandstone which was quarried at Dufton Gill, two miles distant. It was constructed between 1871 and 1874. Barytes, better known perhaps as barium sulphate, used to be mined in the vicinity, and an aerial ropeway once connected the mine to a bunker and hopper located in the goods yard at Long Marton. This installation is thought to have been brought into use in 1941, but it is not known when operations ceased.

Neville Simms

The scene is the somewhat dilapidated station at New Biggin on 15th June 1967, where BR Class 9F No.92056, *en route* from Long Meg sidings to Widnes, has stopped to attach ten more hopper wagons to its train. Note that the wagons being shunted by the 9F are sheeted, whereas those from Long Meg are uncovered. This appears to have been regular practice at this time for reasons unknown to the author – perhaps it depended on the type of mineral being conveyed. New Biggin station lost its general goods facilities in November 1966 and became unstaffed from January 1967. It was closed to passenger traffic in May 1970. New Biggin signal box, which dated from 1890 and lasted until 1973, is partially visible on the left of the picture.

The late Derek Cross

A scene which will be immediately recognised by the overwhelming majority of steam fans! On 11th August 1968 BR, to quote their own publicity, finally 'ran out of steam', and a special train was run from Liverpool to Carlisle and return via Settle to commemorate this melancholy occasion. The train will always be best remembered for the hugely expensive fare demanded, and became known as the 'Fifteen Guinea Special'. On the outward run, the train was hauled over the Settle & Carlisle line by BR Standard 'Britannia' Pacific No.70013 *Oliver Cromwell,* while the return trip was powered by 'Black Five' 4-6-0 locomotives Nos.44871 and 44781, which are seen here passing Culgaith. There was a large number of onlookers even at this comparatively obscure location, while at Ais Gill there were unprecedented crowds and, incredibly, traffic jams on the remote moorland road which passes the summit. Steam traction returned to the line in triumph in 1978, and the Settle & Carlisle line has since become a very popular route for steam-hauled railtours.

The late Derek Cross

An unidentified 'Jubilee' 4-6-0 shatters the rustic peace of Culgaith station, as it hurries northwards with a passenger train on a rather dull August day in 1965. Culgaith was an attractive, well kept station, that had a colourful floral display, but this, unfortunately, did not look its best on the day of this photograph. Note the traditional MR signal box – which replaced an earlier building in 1908 – that controls the level crossing gates, the latter being one of only two level crossings on the entire Settle & Carlisle line. Early MR plans precluded a station at Culgaith, much to the annoyance of the local vicar and some landowners, who protested to MR headquarters at Derby. The MR at first declined their request, but the vicar persisted and it was eventually agreed that a station would be built, with the proviso that the local authority laid a suitable road from the village, which was about 1/4 mile away. The station, which was a totally different design to others on the route, opened on 1st April 1880. Unusually for this line, the platforms were largely of timber construction. No goods yard was provided at Culgaith, only a single siding, which had a small platform for loading purposes.

J. Spencer Gilks

Amidst the beautiful, unspoilt surroundings of the Eden Valley, Class 5MT No.44756, in charge of the 4.36pm Bradford Forster Square to Carlisle stopping train, approaches Armathwaite on 3rd June 1963. The train has just come off the 176 yards long Armathwaite Viaduct, a parapet of which is just visible towards the rear of the train. No.44756, built at Crewe Works in 1948, was equipped with Caprotti valve gear, Timken roller bearings and a double chimney. Other differences to the normal design included the boiler, which was pitched two inches higher than usual, a longer smokebox and the running plate, which was lower than on the standard locomotives. The result was a machine that could hardly be called handsome! For many years No.44756 was allocated to Holbeck shed, and performed on the Settle & Carlisle line on numerous occasions. These Caprotti engines were not at their best climbing gradients however, and were more frequently to be seen south of Leeds. No.44756 was based at Southport towards the end of its career, and was withdrawn from there in October 1964.

R. Leslie

Photographed in low evening sunshine, Fowler Class 4MT 2-6-4T No.42369 leaves Armathwaite with the 6.5pm Carlisle to Appleby local train on 21st May 1963. The coaches, like the engine, are also of LMSR origin. The station's down platform, and stone built shelter, can just be discerned on the left. This train was the return working of the morning Appleby to Carlisle 'local'. In view of the considerable amount of light engine running required to and from Carlisle it is, perhaps, surprising that steam traction was still employed on these workings.

R. Leslie

Class 5MT No.45118 takes an up mixed freight from Carlisle through Armathwaite on the evening of 19th April 1963. The locomotive is in very clean condition, and possibly fresh from an overhaul. On the left of the picture is the small goods yard, which closed on 6th April 1964. No.45118 was one of a batch of 'Black Fives' constructed in 1935 by Vulcan Foundry, and it lasted in traffic until October 1966.

R. Leslie

Another evening shot at Armathwaite, with the 4.36pm Bradford to Carlisle stopping train pulling away from the station: the engine is rebuilt 'Patriot' 4-6-0 No.45535 *Sir Herbert Walker KCB*. No.45535 was originally constructed in 1933, and was rebuilt with a 2A type taper boiler in 1948. It was withdrawn from service five months after this portrait was taken. The passenger accommodation comprises of a set of three LMSR coaches, while the vehicle immediately behind the locomotive is a four wheeled parcels van of Southern Railway design. Like all of the wayside stations on the Settle & Carlisle line, Armathwaite had a poor passenger service of three weekday trains in each direction, which reflected the fact that it only served a tiny village in a sparsely inhabited area with little traffic potential.

R. Leslie

LMSR Class 4F 0-6-0 No.44277 plods wearily uphill near Cotehill with the daily 'pick up' freight from Durran Hill to Skipton on 22nd December 1962. It was a resident of Skipton shed for many years, so it is likely that No.44277 performed this task regularly. The Class 4F still has more than a mile of climbing ahead before the summit is reached, beyond the site of the former Cotehill Station. The station there only served two small hamlets, Cotehill and Knot Hill, and was an early closure casualty, passenger trains being withdrawn as long ago as 7th April 1952. The station buildings and signal box were demolished soon afterwards, and there is now no trace that a station ever existed at that spot.

R. Leslie

Class 5MT No.44677 makes a spirited ascent of the 1 in 132 at Cotehill, with an up express freight from Durran Hill (Carlisle) on 2nd February 1963. The Settle & Carlisle line is famous for the heavy gradients which were necessary to take the line across the Pennines, but inclines such as this, which continues for almost seven miles from Petteril Bridge Junction to just beyond the site of Cotehill station are, perhaps, less well known. No.44677 was one of the last 'Black Fives' to be constructed, emerging from Horwich Works in April 1950.

It was one of a batch of ten locomotives fitted with Skefko roller bearings on the driving axles only. For many years it was allocated to St. Rollox shed, Glasgow, and was selected by the Scottish Region to run paired with a self weighing tender. In about 1962 No.44677 was transferred to Carlisle (Kingmoor) shed, but retained its special tender. At the time of this picture it was also fitted with a snowplough, which helps to make No.44677 a very distinctive machine indeed.

R. Leslie

LNER A3 Class Pacific No.60092 *Fairway* awaits departure from Carlisle with the up 'Waverley' on 30th July 1960. This locomotive had been reallocated from Heaton shed, Newcastle, to Holbeck depot (Leeds) two months previously for working the Scottish expresses over the Settle & Carlisle line, and is seen here in quite clean condition, which was unusual for a Holbeck based A3 Class Pacific! No.60092 remained at Holbeck until June 1961, when it was moved to nearby Ardsley shed. By the following year, *Fairway* was back on Tyneside, but by this time based at Gateshead shed, and had gained German-type smoke deflectors, presumably during a visit to Doncaster Works. It was withdrawn from service in October 1964.

Neil Thexton